The Way of the Living Sword

The Way of the Living Sword

Yagyu Munenori

The Warrior Series: Book Five

D E Tarver

iUniverse, Inc.
New York Lincoln Shanghai

The Way of the Living Sword
Yagyu Munenori

iUniverse, Inc.

For information address:
iUniverse
2021 Pine Lake Road, Suite 100
Lincoln, NE 68512
www.iuniverse.com

ISBN: 0-595-27998-8

Printed in the United States of America

I would like to dedicate this book to all of my teachers, both martial arts and other. The knowledge you have given me has changed my life. I wish I had been a better student.

It is because a mirror has no commitment to any image that it can clearly and accurately reflect any image before it. The mind of a warrior is like a mirror in that it has no commitment to any outcome and is free to let form and purpose result on the spot, according to the situation.

—Yagyu Munenori

CONTENTS

The Way of the Living Sword

The Sword of Death

The Living Sword

No Sword

PREFACE

This book contains the translated writings of Yagyu Munenori, one of the greatest swordsmen who ever lived, founder of the Yagyu Shinkage-ryu style of swordsmanship. Whereas most interpretations of his work are approached from a purely academic angle, I believe my lifetime of experience studying the sword and martial arts gives me a unique and practical perspective on the subject. As those of you who have also studied know, and as Munenori himself would say, you can only understand so much about martial arts from reading.

I was first introduced to Munenori's work about twenty-two years ago, while I was staying in Japan, and I have been an avid student ever since. There are several books on the market that attempt to instruct on both Zen and the martial arts, but this one comes to us from one of the few masters who spent extensive amounts of time studying both disciplines. It is a small book, but the information contained could well take a lifetime to master. In true Japanese fashion, Munenori wrote in a very condensed style—each sentence requires a fair amount of thought and meditation, as well as time spent in physical training, to fully comprehend. I have studied martial arts myself for many years, yet I still find that his work opens me up to higher levels of comprehension.

My advice is to read this book once a week for a month or so, then every month for a few years as you continue to train. Let go of the things that hold you back. Seek truth and accept it as it comes. Study. Practice. Train. Question. Experiment. Grow. Your future is in your own hands. To all warriors from every walk of life, salutations.

D. E. Tarver

Yagyu Munenori

Yagyu Munenori (1571–1646) was without doubt one of the most educated sword masters of all times. He inherited the prestigious position of sword instructor to the Tokugawa family from his famous father at a young age. His writing shows the depth of his learning and understanding of the Zen principles that underline his approach to teaching swordsmanship.

Yagyu Munenori was a contemporary of the famous Musashi, and although the two where among the most elite warriors of their time, it is hard to find two more contrasting lives. Musashi started out a poor outcast and clawed his way to the top, while Munenori benefited from the political dealings of his father and the Tokugawa clan. Be that as it may, he did indeed earn his reputation as a great master/teacher. In one famous duel, he killed seven attackers while protecting the shogun. It just goes to show that the cream will rise to the top no matter where it starts out.

The Way of the Living Sword is one of the most in-depth studies of the connection between the physical martial arts and the mental process of Zen available anywhere. While Munenori and Musashi were both avid students of Zen, I think Munenori was more fascinated by the academic aspects of the philosophy, and his work shows it.

He was an enthusiastic student of the famous Zen master Takuan Soho, to whom he refers as his master in the text. In deference to his teacher, and in typical Japanese style, Munenori refuses to claim any mastery in the Zen teachings, but it is obvious to anyone familiar with Zen and the martial arts that his understanding was very impressive.

Munenori will stretch the consciousness of even the most enlightened martial artist. You will experience many flashes of revelation as you connect with the various aspects of his approach. Of all of the books in the warrior series, I believe that *The Book of Five Rings* and *The Way of the Living Sword* have the foremost ability take readers to the deepest places within themselves. If you are one of the few, you may find yourself among the cream of the top.

About the Title

The original text was called *The Secret Teachings of the Family Sword.* I chose to title this version *The Way of the Living Sword* because I feel that it best captures the dynamic of the text. The secrets are now in your hands, and you will soon be on the path to enlightenment. The more you read it, the more you will understand. In any field of endeavor, only the most diligent students reach expert levels. Determine now to be in that number.

Far too many people "rehash what they have heard but have no real understanding themselves," as Munenori would say. Be the exception.

The Way of the Living Sword

Yagyu Munenori

WWW.DETARVER.COM

THE SWORD OF DEATH

The old warriors said, "Weapons are a necessary evil and Heaven detests them. Use them only when there is no other possibility." It is the nature of Heaven to give life and nourish all things, and any weapon used to kill, whether it is a sword, bow, or *naginata*, is in direct conflict with the will of Heaven. Since these are used to kill Heaven's beloved children, Heaven hates them.

We must also consider that weapons are instruments of Heaven's wrath and judgment. In the natural cycle of things, spring breezes bring life and greenery to the earth, but the winter frost destroys the life that the spring brings. Heaven's love and judgment follow this same path. It makes sense to put a stop to evil because human beings will take advantage of an opportunity to commit evil, and once that evil is revealed it must be judged. For this purpose, weapons are also approved by Heaven.

A single tyrant may kill or torture thousands of innocent people. If you can save the thousands from death or torture, is it not best to kill that one man? In this way, the sword of death is also the sword of life.

It takes an expert to properly handle a weapon, and if you are not well-versed chances are that you will be killed yourself while trying to strike down another.

After careful study you come to realize that in almost all battles or duels of one against one with swords, one will die and only one will live. This is strategy on the smallest scale, and the repercussions are, on the whole, very small.

However, if that one man is a commander, his warriors represent his arms, legs, and fists. Now, if this single man wins or loses, it affects the whole of the state as well as all of his warriors. This is strategy on a much larger scale. If the commander's arms and legs work in a coordinated effort, which is to say if his warriors work well together, he will win. If not, he will lose. This is the same for individual combat. When two warriors cross swords, the one with the best coordination and focus will win. The same is true of the commander, who must coordinate his troops and resources in a focused effort.

Victory and defeat are decided on the field of battle against opposing forces set to destroy one another. The victor will be the commander who can play out various scenarios in his mind and determine the best course for his army. This is the art of strategy.

In times of peace, the art of war is also manifest by concentrating on various disturbances and heading off problems of the state before they spread and grow dangerous. The way to accomplish this is to appoint the right leaders for villages, towns, and provinces. A leader who seeks personal gain at the expense of the populace will quickly start to undermine the security of the state. Building a proper leadership structure is the foundation of the art of war and the first line of defense for the state. Self-interested magistrates are enemies of the peace. Take the lessons of the sword into consideration where one must know not only what is opponent is doing, but what he is about to do. The lessons of sword combat can indeed apply to many situations.

A ruler is often surrounded by scheming manipulators who cast gracious eyes toward the lord but look toward his subjects with a cold stare. Such a person will only give favorable reports of you if you entice them with money or power. In this way even great accomplishments will be presented as evil and the good will suffer while the evil flourish. Your ability to spot this is even more vital than properly reading your opponent in a duel where your life is on the line.

The state and all the people in it are the lord's responsibility. Those close to him serve in the same manner as those who are distant. Proximity is irrelevant in matters of importance. Remember, the lord's servants are the same as his arms and legs; just because the legs are farther from the head, are they less important than the arms? Since they both operate and feel pain alike, what difference does it make which one is farther from the head?

When those who are close to the lord use the situation to take advantage of those at a greater distance, the innocents will suffer and despise the lord. In this way, the lord will be accused of inflecting harm on blameless people, even though he is not responsible. Usually there are no more than five or ten people that have access to a leader; the vast majority of his subjects are at a distance, and they will rise up if they despise the lord. Those close to the lord, who served him all along from a position of self-interest rather than for the good of the land, will be the first to turn on him when times are difficult.

These things can happen because of a leader's assistants and may in no way be the fault of the leader. It is important to understand this from the beginning and make it clear that you wish to extend consideration and benefits even to those at the greatest distances. This understanding is also part of the art of strategy.

In order to engage in successful long-term relations, you must be able to apply your strategy to your companions also. If you do not a conflict may spring up around you, because you are not aware of your surroundings, and if you remain in this situation too long you will end up blamed for something in which you had no part. On the other hand, if you are not fully aware of your surroundings, you will eventually speak out of place, because you haven't read the positions of others, and end up giving your life in some useless quarrel. All of this hinges on your ability to properly read the intentions of others and apply appropriate strategic thinking.

Apply the warrior's strategic thinking to all things, even as basic as the placement of furniture in a room. There is only one truth in all things—it stands apart from human reason—find the truth and stand on it, regardless of your situation. Apply this to leadership and government also.

It is shortsighted to think of sword strategy as simply a means of killing. The man is irrelevant; it is the evil that must be destroyed. Proper strategy will allow thousands to live in peace due to the killing of one evil man.

The things recorded here are only for this house and should not leave. That is not to say that the information should be kept secret from the most worthy students. If knowledge is not passed on it is useless. Let my descendants consider this well.

Enlightenment

The attainment of enlightenment in strategy is like a gate to the entrance of a home. When you reach the gate you know that the home is near, but you must pass through the gate to reach the house and meet the host.

Education is the gateway to enlightenment, but it is not the house. When you reach the gate do not think you have reached enlightenment. To reach enlightenment you must pass through the gate and enter the house. Books are tools to help you reach your destination, not your destination themselves. Do not make the mistake of many by thinking that reading many books will open your mind to the way of things. No amount of education or book learning alone can bring one true understanding, no matter how many facts they state.

Those who rely on these things are often well-versed in the classics and the writings of great masters, but they cannot think for themselves. A certain amount of education is helpful, but highly-educated orators may know nothing of truth even though they talk big, swelling words and seem self-assured. There are those who walk the path of truth all of their lives and appear born with a certain enlightenment, though they have never received any education.

Universal Enlightenment is the state of understanding the way of all things and using that understanding to accomplish anything. Understanding the way of all things is to exist as one with the way and the spirit of everything in existence, to be at one with your environment and accomplish anything with your awareness of, and insight into, the way. When you reach the limit of your understanding in the way you also reach the limit of your ability. If you have not reached enlightenment you can really do nothing of your own.

At first your mind stops at many points in a process because of your uncertainty, and action is hindered because of reason. Once enlightened, your mind is liberated from thought and you are free to react to any situation naturally and instantly. When you first set out to learn a martial art, your mind is free and clear of hindrances. But after you have learned a little you question and reason, and your mind grows encumbered with many things, and even the smallest actions seem impossible. After you have mastered the art your mind is no longer engaged and you are free to complete even the most difficult techniques or tasks with ease. At this point you are one with your art and you understand the strategy of the way, and everything you do flows naturally from your spirit with perfection.

The techniques of the sword consist of hundreds of cuts, stances, postures, and eye positions. Once you have learned all there is to learn of your art and you continue to practice the same things over and over until they become part of you, they then disappear from your mind and your mind is freed from the process, content, and details of the sword.

After you have polished your forms with continued practice, your hands, feet, and body act according to the situation and your mind never enters into this at all. The forms cease to exist and the techniques disappear, yet your every move is in perfect harmony with them. Once you reach this level of enlightenment you are completely unaware of your mind and even devils of the air cannot read your intentions. The forms exist for the purpose of bringing you to this level, and the circle is complete when they disappear from your thoughts and become part of your soul.

This is the philosophy of Zen and the goal of all martial arts and disciplines. Learn to forget what you have learned. Discipline your mind to free your mind from discipline. Become one with the universal enlightenment of all things and accomplish everything with no thought to anything. The ultimate goal of all learning is to forget all that you have learned.

Mind and Spirit

That part inside each of us that makes plans, determines actions, and commits us to a path is called the mind. That part inside each of us that carries out plans, fulfills actions, and walks the path is called the spirit. The mind is the ultimate master of the body, and the spirit is its servant, to carry out the directions of the mind. The mind uses the spirit to accomplish all that it does. If the spirit acts too much on its own, you will fail. Insure that you commit all things to your mind and strive to bring your spirit under subjection of your mind and the two will work as a seamless duo.

In martial arts, for example, readying your stance is a function of the mind. To block, parry, and strike in the heat of battle is a function of your spirit. However intense the battle, if you allow your spirit to take control you will lose your stance and have no power. In order to survive you must keep your fighting spirit under the strict discipline of your mind, otherwise you risk following your spirit into intense battle and leaving behind your techniques, knowledge, and training.

Deception

All fighting is based on deception. Deception is the art of showing your opponent one thing while you are doing or about to do another, leading the opponent in a false direction in order to gain victory.

Remain alert, know when your opponent is trying to set you up; if you are not aware of his deception you will be drawn into his timing and destroyed. If you are trying to set up your opponent and he follows you, lead him to his death. If he catches on to what you are doing, immediately change direction and cut him down. In this way your original deception will work because it allowed you to set him up for the finishing blow.

Deception is essentially the same in all areas even though it carries a different name.

In Buddhism it is known as the means. By keeping your truth inside and showing a person only what he is ready for, you can eventually lead him into the whole truth. Therefore, deception is a strategy for winning converts.

In Shintoism it is known as a mystery. By keeping the spirit world mysterious and beyond knowing you can inspire faith in a person, and once he has faith everyone around him will benefit from it.

In the path of the warrior it is known simply as strategy. Creating a false impression in your opponent and deceiving him, even though it is a lie, is ultimately a virtue if in the end you win without harming him. This is known as using evil for good.

Beat the Grass to Scare the Snakes

A Zen parable says, "Beat the grass to scare the snakes." One use of deception is to startle or shock your opponent, just as you would scare away snakes by striking the tall weeds and bushes.

Doing that which your opponent least expects in order to startle him is an excellent use of strategy. By startling him, you will shock his nervous system and overload his senses. This will cause a gap between his mind and actions. Even something as simple as throwing your arms about can draw him out of his timing.

Strategy may also include indifferently tossing your sword aside, if you are enlightened in the swordless art, and using your opponent's sword against him. In this case, you are the master of your opponent's sword. This is snatching opportunity out of the instant.

Snatching Opportunity out of the Instant

To snatch opportunity out of the instant is to be at one with the moment. Before your opponent commits to an action his spirit will direct him. You must be able to read beneath the surface and accurately interrupt your opponent's intentions. Use the opportunity between his spirit's command and his physical commitment to action.

This is the purest form of Zen philosophy and is taught in the doctrine of dynamics.

Intent is born in the mind and hidden in the spirit. It is like the tracks of a door hidden on the inside. Although you cannot see the tracks, you take hold of the door knowing it will open. Using this same strategy in combat is known as snatching opportunity out of the instant.

The Principles of First Strike and Counterstrike

First strike is when you commit everything you have—mind, body, and spirit— into the initial attack of an opponent, with every move, cut, and tactic at your disposal, in an attempt to deliver the first cardinal strike. The principle of first strike is the same whether you or your opponent employs it.

The principle of counterstrike is that you assume a guard instead of attacking and wait for your opponent to make the first move. You must remain very alert when using the counterstrike method.

As we see, the principles of first strike and counterstrike are really the strategy of attacking or waiting.

The idea of counterstrike is based on drawing the opponent in. To accomplish this, you may leave an opening in your guard so that the opponent sees a clear strike at your body. Tempt the opponent with the thought of an easy victory, and when he makes his move use his commitment to counter him. In this instance your stance is in a first-strike posture, but your sword is set to counterstrike when the opponent advances. The whole purpose of creating an opening for your opponent is to set him up for the counter.

This strategy requires your mind and your body. Your body should take a first-strike posture, but your mind must remain resolved and calm, waiting to deliver the counter strike. If you let your thoughts run ahead of you they will try to anticipate your opponent and throw your timing off. This can be very dangerous. You must discipline your mind to wait for the opponent's full commitment to an aggressive action. If you do not control your mind you will lose, because you will try to kill the opponent.

This strategy also works by keeping the mind aggressive and the body relaxed. In order to do this correctly, you must keep your mind tense while making your body appear defenseless, thus causing your opponent to make the first commitment.

The Body, in this context, should be considered the hands that hold the sword. Even though this strategy can be used both ways, the bottom line is to induce your opponent to commit to action first.

Instructions for Fighting an Aggressive Opponent

First, carefully read the opponent by studying his posture and attitude. Notice how he places his hands on the sword and the bend in his arms. Watch his chest and shoulders to observe how he moves. These are difficult lessons to learn and can really be taught only in person.

Next, consider your own body, how you grip the sword and your stance. Pay close attention to the three essentials of timing, distancing, and positioning. Keep your mind steady but flexible.

This next part is completely beyond learning from a book. You can come to understanding only by taking sword in hand and engaging an opponent. But for the record I will list them here.

- Using your fists as a shield
- Coordinating your body posture with your opponent's
- Squaring your shoulders with your opponent's hands
- Modifying your stance by extending your rear leg
- Mirroring your opponent's postures and guard no matter what he does

It is absolutely necessary to prepare yourself by daily practice. Rehearse the proper stances, cuts, and guards until you embed them in your mind. If you wait until you are actually in combat before you consider these things, your mind will be unsettled and even the basics will not work for you.

Instructions for Fighting a Reflexive Opponent

Again, pay close attention to how he holds the sword and bends his arms, and watch his chest and shoulders to see how he moves. These three things are important to observe when fighting an aggressive opponent, but they are particularly important when facing a reflexive opponent.

These three areas are essential for reading an opponent. When you are attacking, watch your opponent's arms. When in the midst of dueling, watch his chest and shoulders. And you should strive to always be aware of his hands.

Instructions for Fighting an Opponent Who is Hard to Read

At times you will come across an opponent who is almost impossible to read. In this instance there are three techniques you can try to cause him to indicate his intentions. These work well whether the opponent is aggressive or waiting.

1. Change and adapt to change. When an opponent is in a waiting stance it is often possible to draw out his intentions by making deliberate and calculated changes to see how he will respond. Change your body position or strategy and seamlessly adapt to his adjustments.

2. See without looking. As you try various changes you should watch the reaction of the opponent without looking directly at him. Keep your eyes moving as though you have noticed nothing of importance. Use dashing glances and peripheral vision to take in all that the opponent is doing without appearing to see anything he is doing. A line in a poem reads, "Without looking, the dragonfly sees, and escapes the shrike." Just like the dragonfly, you must remain fully aware of your opponent's every move without looking at him or revealing your own intentions. Dramatic actors use a similar technique where they glance once then shift their eyes back without staring.

3. Allow the opponent to strike then kill him. Give your opponent an obvious target and allow him to slash at it. Know your distance and timing and the strike will pass harmlessly by. The more determined he is to cut you down, the more exposed he will be. Regardless of his intentions or determination, you control the situation by controlling the distance and timing. The sword that does not hit its target brings death to its master. As soon as the blade passes, lunge forward and cut him down. If you miss, cut again and again. Do not allow your opponent to so much as raise his hands, or by missing you will give him the same opportunity to kill you. In a duel with swords the first to hesitate will die. Do not allow your mind to stop on any point. If you contemplate why you missed, you will die with the same thought in your mind and your whole strategy will have worked against you. Do not concern yourself with cutting the opponent. Let the sword continually follow its own path over and over without allowing your opponent to as much as look in your direction. Life or death is decided by a single cut.

The Three Timings

There are three types of timing to consider. One is when you and your opponent strike each other at the same instant. Next is when you come underneath the opponent's raised sword and strike him. And then comes when you strike your opponent high while his sword is low.

Do not allow yourself to be drawn into the opponent's timing. If you synchronize your timing to his, he is in control of the fight. You must force him to match your timing so that you can control the fight. Whichever of you has control of the timing has superior use of his blade. Regardless of your strategy, do not allow your opponent to control your timing. If you do you will be at a serious disadvantage.

Use Opposing Timing

If your opponent attacks with a fast timing you should counter with a slow timing. If your opponent attacks with a slow timing you should counter with a fast timing. Again, we see the principle of controlling the timing rather than allowing the opponent the advantage of control.

Take the singer and the drummer, for example. An accomplished singer chants in broken patterns and it is very difficult for a novice drummer to play properly. Trying to match a talented singer with a novice drummer or a talented drummer with a novice singer will make it very difficult for them to act in unison.

This same principle is true for the swordsman and is known as the art of erratic timing. If the singer sings slowly the drummer cannot play a quick beat—it will sound dreadful. If the singer sings loud and quickly, a gentle drummer will ruin the song.

An expert bird catcher makes sure the bird sees his pole from a distance. He moves it slowly and draws the bird into his timing until he is close enough to catch it. The bird, caught up in the timing of the swaying pole, flaps its wings and hovers, but is unable to break the spell of the swaying pole. Once drawn into the bird catcher's timing the bird is easily caught.

Likewise, it is necessary for you to control the timing of the fight and avoid being drawn into your opponent's timing. If you control the timing and distance, you can strike your opponent at will. The art of erratic timing is a study of its own.

Understanding the Way of Timing

The singer and musician must know the timing of the music before playing the first note, or else they will be out of sync. Fighting is no different. You must be able to read the intentions of your opponent by his subtle movements and handling of his sword. See what he is going to do by understanding what he is doing. Perfect this skill to the same level as master musicians and singers and you will be able to strike your opponent at will.

Six Primary Rules for Combat

1. When the opponent strikes he is vulnerable.
2. A three-inch advantage is enough to win.
3. Maintain a distance no more than the opponent's height and you will be able to close the distance in a flash to strike.
4. Watch the opponent's elbows when he is in an upper guard.

5. When the opponent is making big moves concentrate on his center.

6. With a three-foot distance you can strike the opponent without adjustment.

It is impossible to properly learn these techniques from reading about them, so I did not waste a lot of time writing them in detail. You must practice these under the supervision of your sensei in order to perfect them.

If you have exhausted every technique and strategy available to you but your opponent is unmoved and remains in a defensive guard, refusing to make the first move, try crowding him by moving within three feet of him. If you do this properly he will feel the pressure of an attack, even though you are not attacking, and take an offensive guard. Induce him to make the first strike and use the opening to kill him.

If the opponent refuses to strike first it will be hard to kill him. Keep in mind that you must master the proper use of distance, timing, and evasion in order to properly use this strategy. If you do not, you will be cut down without ever seeing the sword that killed you. Once you have mastered this maneuver, use it without fear or hesitation. Move in on your opponent and force him to strike, and then take his life. This is how you think several steps ahead of your opponent.

Four Overall Strategies

1. Overall deception and opening moves. Must be explained in person.

2. Keep your mind open and clear at all times in both offensive and defensive modes. Must be explained in person.

3. The short sword by seventeen inches.

4. Use both offensive and defensive modes by placing your body in an offensive guard while holding your sword in a defensive posture.

You must look to your sensei for proper instruction on these strategies. It is not possible to learn them from a book.

Hear the Wind Listen to the Water

The point of all strategic study is to win by causing your opponent to commit to a wrong move. Use whatever tactics or strategy you must in order to entice him into making the first strike. Change guards, feign strikes, and shift strategies.

Approach the fight with the thought that your opponent will be the aggressor and pay close attention to his subtle movements. The proper state of mind is the key to victory. If you do not assume that your opponent will attack aggressively, you will be caught off guard if he launches a fierce attack, and all of your training and study will evaporate the second the fight begins. Set your mind on killing him and your body and stance will take an aggressive posture, but make sure you keep your sword in a ready defensive posture. Read your opponent's intentions and use them against him. Make his knowledge your own. If you cannot read these things with a clear mind, all of your training is for nothing.

"Hear the wind listen to the water" means to remain calm and serene outwardly even when a fierce fighting spirit is raging within. Wind is completely silent. Sound comes only when the wind strikes other objects. The wind in the sky is silent. When the wind comes against trees or bamboo it then creates a loud and violent sound. Likewise, water falling from the sky makes no sound until it strikes things below, and then it can sound thunderous.

Be like the wind and the water, completely calm and silent to the observer but with a fierce fighting spirit set on a trigger beneath. You should appear peaceful and unconcerned on the surface even as you are set to instantly react on the inside.

It is a bad thing to allow your body to rush the movements of your hands and feet. You must approach a fight with a duality of aggression and defense, one of the body and the other of the spirit. It is dangerous to allow your whole being to get caught up in aggression or defense. Consider the yin and yang as a model. Aggression is yang and defense is yin. As one spirit moves to the surface, allow the other to settle below. When aggression moves outward your mind must remain calm and defensive. When you are calm and defensive outwardly, your spirit must remain aggressively ready to strike down the opponent at any second.

In the study of the sword you set your mind like a spring trap and keep your body resting and peaceful. Yin and yang in this regard is in complete accord with Heaven's design.

Remember, if you remain calm and clear on the inside even though you are attacking with intense violence on the outside, you will remain in control of your movements. If you allow your whole self to get carried away with aggression or defense, you will not have command of your techniques. Keep the spirit and the body working separately but in accord with a proper balance of aggression and defense. Both mind and body have separate jobs, but they should work in unison as though they are one and the same.

A duck on the water appears to rest although its feet are busily working beneath the surface. Strive to do likewise in your training. Once you have mastered this knowledge and completed the circle there will be no inside or outside, and you will be at one with your training and environment and strike without effort. This state is the highest level of enlightenment.

Affliction

To be fixated only with the thought of winning is an affliction of the mind. The same is true of one fixated with the thought of using his skill, or testing every little technique, or being preoccupied with aggression or defense rather than a balance of both. It is also an affliction for one to become obsessed with freeing himself of these afflictions. Anything that dominates the mind to the exclusion of other things is an affliction of the mind. Since all of the afflictions are in the mind, you will not reach excellence until you are rid of them.

Beginning and Advanced Stages of Cleansing the Mind of Affliction

Beginning Stages

In the beginning, you must fixate your mind on getting rid of fixations. The thought of ridding oneself of thought is itself a thought and a stopping point in the mind.

Thought is a burden of the mind; nevertheless, to rid the mind of thought we must first self-impose an intentional burden and thus bombard the mind with thought. The very desire to free the mind of obsessive thought is an obsessive thought. So we use thought to rid ourselves of thought. Once you are free from thought your mind will be free even of the desire to free the mind.

It is like using a wedge to free another wedge. When a wedge is stuck so that you cannot free it by any other means you take a second wedge and drive it in beside the first in order to free them both. The same is true of the mind. You think in order to free the mind of all thought and in the end the thought you forced in will also disappear.

Obsession is used to cancel out obsession and in the end the mind is free from all attachments and stopping points.

Advanced Stages

In the advanced stages the mind protects itself from obsession by having no thought of obsession. The thought of thought is a thought. To operate in the midst of obsession without giving thought to obsession is to be free from obsession.

The thought of freeing your mind from obsession comes because the mind is obsessed with the thought of being free. The thought of being rid of thought is a stopping point for the mind and you can move no further until you are free of it.

Use the beginning and advanced stages to accomplish the overall objective. Constantly apply the strategies of the beginning stage and eventually all the thoughts and stopping points of the mind will fade away with no direct effort on your part.

Obsession is an attachment of the mind, a stopping point. Buddhists loathe attachment. A monk who is free of attachment is free to mingle with everyone without becoming entangled in their attachments because his mind flows freely without thought to any attachments whatsoever.

No master is attached to his art. They must leave attachment behind and allow the art to happen of its own accord. A rough-cut diamond collects dust and dirt in the creases, but a highly polished diamond does not. A polished diamond will sparkle even if it is covered in mud.

Polish your mind so that it sparkles. Free it from all obsessions, thought, and stopping points and you may do as you please with out affliction.

The Free Mind

A monk once asked an ancient man of stature, "What is the Way?"

The man said, "The Way of the free mind."

This lesson applies to all arts. The ultimate achievement of any mind is to attain the state of freedom. A free mind is one free of affliction, living in clear reaction even in the midst of all afflictions. Let us take an example from everyday life. When drawing a bow, if you are aware of the arrow it will be very difficult to hit the target. If you are aware of the sword in your hand it will become difficult to control. If you are aware of the brush in your hand your writing will be shaky and unsteady. If you are aware of the musical instrument the music will be off beat and out of tune.

The archer must forget the arrow. When he shoots the bow with the same mind as when he is doing nothing at all he will be much more accurate. Wielding a sword, riding a horse, or playing a musical instrument should all be done without thought to anything. The mind should remain in a state of rest no matter the activity. Use the sword as though you are not using the sword. Ride the horse as though you are not riding a horse, and play music as though you are not playing. Separate your mind from the activity and release all effort. Do everything as though you are doing nothing and everything will happen of its own accord, smoothly and easily.

Whatever your path, if you set out with determination to accomplish your goal, you are not following the Way of the free mind. When you follow your path without a burning desire to control the outcome you are in accord with the Way. Commit to the action of the instant without thought or desire, and you will accomplish all things without effort.

It is because a mirror has no commitment to any image that it can clearly and accurately reflect any image before it. The mind of a warrior is like a mirror in that it has no commitment to any outcome and is free to let form and purpose result on the spot, according to the situation.

The state of a free mind is evident in a warrior who can accomplish all things with no thought to anything. Such a one is rightly called a master.

No matter what you set out to accomplish, if you engage the project determined to control the outcome you will be confused and confounded throughout. Some things will go well for you, and when you think you have the key to understanding other things will go badly. It may be that you do something well twice before it goes badly one time. If you are happy they it went well twice, you will think that you are onto something, but then it will go badly again. This is because you are trying to force the outcome by applying the same tactics to every situation in stead of letting every situation flow of its own accord.

Over time, after many successes and failures have built up and the desire to control the outcome fades, you will begin to do everything more efficiently. The desire to control will give way to the idea that success is random, and you will then let situations flow of their own accord. At this point, you will release your mind and desire and you will make no mistakes out of ten accomplishments. Even at this advanced stage, if you see your success and attempt to control the end you will start making mistakes again.

Learn to react to situations without regard to outcome or thought or desire. The state of no thought is not a state without thinking. It is simply a state where the mind and body are free to react instantly, without hesitation.

A Man Made of Wood

Layman Pang said, "Be like a man made of wood facing flowers and birds." The idea is that a wooden man's mind will not be moved by the sight of birds or flowers or anything else before him, because he has no mind. It makes perfect sense that a wooden man is not moved, but how can a real man remain unmoved like a wooden figure?

The idea of the wooden man is a metaphor. It is impossible for a real man with a heart and mind to become exactly like a man made of wood. Flesh and blood cannot turn into wood or bamboo. The lesson to learn here is that although you see the flower, your mind does not reconstruct the images of flowers, and you are free to absorb the beauty of the flower you see with no conscious thought to the flower. The free mind is one in essence with the flower rather than standing back in awe of it.

Now, when you release an arrow you should have no conscious thought of the arrow or the bow. The free mind is not aware of the bow, the arrow or the target. It does not try to shoot; it simply allows it to happen without stirring or trying to control the arrow. A free mind is not bound by thought or desire. If your mind is aware of the arrow you will be unsettled by desire and will be troubled both inside and out. Anything done with an unsettled mind will not be true to the way it should be.

To reply correctly without the mind searching for answers is awe-inspiring and praiseworthy. It is said that to become a master one must have a free mind.

Reaching the State of the Free Mind

Master Chungfeng said, "At one with a free mind." Reaching this level requires that you go through two stages.

If you free your mind it will find its own stopping point, and you must force it to come back to you so that it can continue to be free. For example, if you cut some-one with the sword, your mind will be impressed at the sight and stop. You must force it to come back to you in order to continue.

At the advanced level, you release the mind and it will not stop at any point. You are able to free the mind after you have trained it not to stop anywhere without having to force it back. Once you have trained your mind not to stop it would be an intrusion on the mind to force it anywhere. To be at one with a free mind means that even though the mind is totally free it does not linger anywhere. It has no need of supervision and is in complete unison with the body.

Once your mind is free you can react to your environment and situation instantly. So long as you are aware of a need to tether your mind, it is not free. You cannot properly raise a tethered cat or dog; they must be freed to grow the way they should.

A student of Confucian thought ties himself to the concept of remaining focused, thinking that focus is necessary for self-improvement; in reality, they cannot grow beyond this elementary thought. Their minds are like cats that have been raised on a short leash.

Buddhism also teaches a devotion to single-minded focus. In the single-minded focus of paying respect to the Buddha, the Buddhists are the same as the Confucians.

These are attempts to free a troubled mind of other thought, but a truly free mind is not troubled in the first place. The beginner recites, "Great immovable teacher," and strives the hold their body and hands in a perfect position while their minds concentrate on the image of the great teacher. This is done to coordinate the mind, body, and spirit in equal measure, and is the same in essence as the Confucian idea of single-minded focus.

The difference is that the effort to coordinate the mind, body, and spirit is only temporary, and as soon as the student ceases the exercise the mind returns to the same easily-distressed state that it was in before.

The master who has truly freed his mind does not have to continually coordinate the mind, body, and spirit. His mind continues to move at all times, yet is immovable at all times. The moon dances on ten thousand waves at once yet does not move. The same is true of the free mind of a master.

I have written this in order to pass on the instruction of my master.

THE LIVING SWORD

Of the hundreds of strategies, postures, and cuts available to master, it is always only one that cuts down the opponent. Regardless of the cuts or defenses used to win, the way of victory is in accurately reading the intentions and ability of your opponent, perceiving his heart and soul.

Even if you know a thousand intricacies of the sword—of stances, guards, cuts and strikes—and are able to teach them all proficiently, it is still the ability to read your opponent's intentions that is at the heart of every victory.

The same is true of your opponent. His knowledge of countless techniques and his years of training and teaching every subtlety of the sword are useless if he can not read the heart and soul of his opponent.

This is a secret of our family sword and is to be taught in person to only the most trusted students. For this reason I will not write about it in any detail or with any clarity in this book.

The Visible and the Invisible

In the way of the sword there are visible and invisible forces, and both are inter-dependent and equal in the reaction of combat and the accurate reading of your opponent's intentions and abilities. The visible are the physical actions of the opponent, his posture, guard, grip, stances and such. The invisible are the things that are not apparent, his intentions, strategy, mind, soul, heart, fighting spirit and such. It's all in the hand that wields the blade. In religion they teach of the physical and the spiritual. The same idea applies here.

Anyone can see the visible, but only the master can see the invisible. The master uses the visible and invisible equally and interchangeably and they control the movements of his blade. If the visible presents itself he will strike, and if the invisible presents itself he will strike. The master will strike according to the opportunity presented the instant it is created, without thought to visible or invisible. When an invisible opportunity presents itself you should strike without waiting for conformation from the visible, and when the visible presents itself you should strike without waiting for conformation from the invisible. Therefore we say the visible and invisible are relevant and equal.

A writing of the Lao Tzu contains the idea of the always visible and always invisible. For every visible that exist there is also an invisible, and the visible and invisible can change places at any time.

When a duck is swimming on top of the water it is visible, but if it dives beneath the surface it becomes invisible. Thus, the things that are commonly considered visible can be hidden and made invisible, and the things that are commonly considered invisible can be read and made visible. Thus we see that visible and invisible are interchangeable and only relevant according to one's ability to read both accurately. With this understanding we can see how visibility and invisibility are interdependent and equal in form, force, and existence.

In religion they also teach of physical reality and spiritual reality. Upon death, the physical reality becomes spiritual reality. Upon birth, the spiritual reality becomes physical reality. Both of the states exist side by side and the reality is the same whether it is manifest physically or spiritually.

These same forces are at play in the hand that wields the blade. This is to be taught in secret to trusted students only. This is the art of reading the visible and the invisible. If you hold something in a closed hand, it is invisible, even though it is there. When you open your hand it is visible, but no more real than it was before. This is more easily explained in person.

If an opening is created visibly you strike accordingly, and if an opening is created invisibly you strike accordingly. That is why I say that these two states exist equally and interchangeably. That which is visible can be invisible and that which is invisible can be visible. These two states are one and the same, and if you fail to read both equally and accurately you will die on the spot regardless of how many techniques you know.

Every form of combat rests on this knowledge.

The Moon Reflecting off the Water

Maintain the proper distancing in a fight to stay out of range of your opponent's sword. Learn to control the distance and close the gap at will to strike the opponent. This technique is known as the moon on the water, because the moon touches the water from a distance.

You should face your opponent like the moon faces the water. Determine and control the distance before the fight even begins. Distancing can only be taught under the supervision of a qualified teacher.

The Resting Sword

This is a matter of high importance. Your body has a natural resting posture, and here we are referring to the natural resting place of the blade itself in conjunction to the body. Whether it is held to your right or left, the blade will find its natural resting place.

Now, when we refer to your opponent, the same word that is used to mean the resting place of your sword also means to comprehend the resting place of the opponent's sword. This is not to be underestimated, because before you can charge your opponent and cut him down you must have a complete awareness of his sword's natural resting place and a comprehension of what it means. This is why we read the characters in two different ways.

The Spirit and the Power

The spirit is on the inside, but is discernible outwardly as power. Take, for example, the life of a tree. The life is on the inside, but it is detectable outwardly because of the blossoms and fragrance they produce and the green leaves on every branch. This is a marvelous thing. Even if you cut the tree open you cannot see the life that produces this marvel of blossoms and green leaves.

In the same way, the spirit of a man cannot be seen or located even if you disassemble him into his smallest parts, but it is because of this invisible force that a man is able to perform all manner of tasks and actions.

When the spirit is still and the sword is resting, all manner of perfect techniques are ready to blossom like flowers in the heat of combat. The spirit works with the mind. It resides deep within, serving the mind to direct the movements of the body, and the mind employs the power of the spirit to concentrate force, *ki*. If the free mind which uses the spirit for power were to stop at any one point, its overall effect would be greatly diminished. For this reason, it is important to insure that the mind continues to move freely.

As an example, imagine the master of a house sending a servant out on an errand. What if the servant reaches the destination and stays where he is and does not return? How then can the master use him further? The mind is the same way. If in the employ of the master the mind stops or even lingers on any one point it will not be at his command for further tasks, and the prowess of the master will diminish.

With this in mind, remember that a free mind is of utmost importance in all that we do, not just in combat. This is an important lesson of both the mind and the spirit.

Movement

Your movement should not be too fast or too slow. Your mind should not engage in the process of your movements. Steps should be natural and without effort. Maintain a proper distance. To rush in too close or to remain too far back are equally disadvantageous and telling. If you rush in too close too quickly you are anticipating the opponent's moves and are not centered. If you stay too far away and move slowly you are afraid and intimidated by the opponent.

It is best to remain disconnected from the process and let your mind move freely.

It is normal for the eyes to blink when something flashes close to them. This is normal and is not a sign of one being upset or flustered. If something is flashed before the eyes several times in an attempt to unsettle someone and they do not blink, the person is already unsettled. A person who is concentrating his effort not to blink has disrupted the state of the free mind. If he were in a state of the free mind he would blink without even knowing it; thus, blinking can be an indication of his readiness.

The point here is to keep your mind open and moving. To resist movement is the same in the mind as moving improperly.

To operate in the natural state of a free mind means that your appearance will not change and your mind will not linger on any one thing.

The Principle of First Reactions

The principle of first reactions is a study of the reactions of the mind when standing face to face with an opponent, or in extreme measures, such as facing an opponent with a spear when you are unarmed.

Most important are your natural or first reactions in a dangerous situation. Anything can happen and your mind is free to go where it will. Where does it go? The idea is to focus the actions of the mind to make sure you are never caught off guard.

First reactions are most clear in the intense moment when you actually cross swords with an opponent in combat, or when the point of the opponent's spear is leveled only a foot and a half from your heart, or when an aggressive opponent has you backed into a corner.

First reactions are vital at times of high intensity. If, when you face an opponent's blade unarmed or are pressed into a corner with no retreat, you allow your mind to pause by concentrating your attention too closely on any one thing, you will not survive.

This is known as the principle of first reactions and is a secret of the masters.

The Principle of One Foot

When your opponent's sword is the same length as yours, you should approach the situation in the same manner as if you were unarmed.

For maximum control you should keep your opponent's sword one foot away from your body. Within this space you are free to maneuver, but to come any closer is very dangerous.

The Principle of the Supreme First Sword

The term "supreme" here refers to the highest level of human perception attainable. The term "first sword" here does not really refer to a blade at all, but to one's ability to read his opponent's intentions and subtle actions. This term is only familiar to those who have entered the secret levels of training. In combat, the principle of first sword is crucial to achieving a quick and decisive victory, because knowing what your opponent is trying to do you can cut him off with a killing strike as he is trying to carry out his strategy.

The ability to read an opponent's intentions and subtle actions is considered first sword, and the sword that reacts seamlessly and instantly to his actions is known as second sword. Set this as your foundation and free your blade to react to whatever attack you receive.

The principles of The Living Sword, The Moon Reflecting off the Water, The Resting Sword, and The Spirit and the Power are four different areas that require understanding. When you add the coordinated movements of the arms, legs, hands, and feet, independent and dependant, this makes five areas that require understanding. All five of these should be seen as one area of study; however, it is important to break them down to the areas of physical seeing and spiritual intuition. What we look at with the eyes is known as physical seeing, while those things that are invisible to the eyes are called intuition. While physical seeing and intuition are two different things, we use them equally to see or create one perception of what is happening around us.

The Living Sword, The Moon Reflecting off the Water, The Resting Sword, The Spirit and the Power, and the movements of the arms, legs, hands, and feet are five areas that combine into one to deliver the overall effect of perceiving and reacting. Although most of what we perceive is through sight, it is the interpretation of what we see that makes mastery of these areas a mental function.

One is a physical attribute and four are spiritual and mental attributes, but they are all one perception.

The Overall Strategy

The Moon Reflecting off the Water is the strategy of understanding and using the physical location of the fight. The Resting Sword is the strategy of body positioning. The movements of the arms, legs, hands, and feet is the strategy of reacting to every movement of your opponent with an appropriate and instant reaction of your own. The purpose of freeing your mind is to perceive accurately and interpret the five areas that make up the one perception of your opponent and surroundings, whether visible or invisible.

Freeing your mind from the sickness of thought is to attain the ability to properly read your opponent's intentions and subtle movements. As long as your mind is bound by the burden of thought, you are apt to miss critical information and lose. If you lose, you die.

By sickness of thought, I mean that which causes the mind to stop on any single point. Strive to free the mind from tarry even at the point where you cut down the opponent.

You must learn to free the mind while keeping it under control.

Three Things to Remember in Combat

1. If your opponent takes a guard with the tip of his sword pointing at your face, cut him down the instant he raises it to cut at you. The best way to set your opponent up is to make him think he can hit you—when he strikes at you he is as good as dead.

2. Take your guard at the optimum distance from your opponent and free your mind to react. If your opponent takes the guard first, don't worry about it; it is the work of the mind that is important here. If your opponent moves five feet, you move five feet, maintaining the optimum distancing at all times. Do not worry about who takes the guard first—focusing on this can be a dangerous distraction. It is far more important to keep your mind free and your body agile.

3. The movement of your feet and the positioning of your body should always take into account the principle of the Resting Sword. This should be a priority before the fight even starts.

Three Steps in Seeing the Resting Sword

The ability to see with your mind is the first step in seeing. Your mind must know what to look for and how to interpret it, then the eyes can see the things the mind is looking for. The eyes serve the mind. First your eyes see, then the mind sees, and the body and limbs react.

Seeing with your body and limbs is to key your body and limbs into the resting place of the opponent's sword. To see with the mind allows the eyes to see and the body and limbs to react and take advantage of the resting sword.

The Reflecting Mind

The Mind is the Moon on the Water
The Body is the Reflection in a Mirror

This represents the essence of a warrior in combat, since the water shows the reflection of the moon and the mirror the reflection of a body. The warrior mind reflects instantly and completely, just as the entire moon appears on the surface of a puddle. The resting sword is like the puddle, and the mind of the warrior is like the moon. The mind of the warrior is read in the resting place of his sword. Let your mind and body become one with the Resting Sword. The body serves the mind.

Also, let the mirror represent the resting sword and allow your body to conform to it like a reflection in a mirror. Your limbs must be at one in time and place with the Resting Sword.

The moon's light strikes the surface of the water the instant it is free of clouds even though it is very far away. The light does not move slowly or in steps to the surface of the water. It is there before the twinkling of an eye, and a warrior's mind is likewise as quick as light from the moon.

The Buddhists say that the free mind is as quick as the moon's reflection on water and the appearance of a reflection in a mirror. Even though the full image of the moon is on the water, the moon itself is still very far away; only the reflection is there instantly. The same is true of a reflection in a mirror—instant reaction without hesitation.

The warrior mind works as fast as a reflection. In the twinkling of an eye you can travel around the world in your mind. As soon as you close your eyes in sleep you instantly create whole worlds in your dreams.

For the warrior, this comparison of the moon on the water is even more appropriate. Allow your mind to take in the whole of the situation, like the puddle reflecting the entire moon. What your mind comprehends your body will react to. As soon as a fight begins you should allow your mind to position your body in the most appropriate position, according to the posture of the opponent, and react to his every move as smoothly and quickly as a reflection reacts to the movements of the person who casts it.

If you do not train your mind beforehand it will not function readily in combat. Free your reactions to the dictates of your mind and allow your arms, hands, feet, and legs to move swiftly and speedily.

Rash Attacks

To make a rash attack is the most dangerous thing a warrior can do. Speed is good, but only after you are completely aware of the whole of the situation and your body works in complete reaction to the opponent. A rash attack will lead to an anxious mind, which is a very bad thing.

Reclaiming the Mind

The idea here is that when you are in the heat of battle and you land a blow, do not allow your mind to hesitate on it. If your mind pauses because of the victory of a single blow, it will cease to function freely. When the mind ceases to function freely, even though you achieved the first blow, the opponent will cut you down because you are no longer free to react to him. Thus, the excitement in the mind over a small victory will cost you a severe loss.

It is particularly important to keep the proper free mind after you wound the opponent. Watch his reaction and be ready to counter. It is common for a wounded opponent to become angry and attack intensely, and if you are not prepared he may overwhelm you. You must see a wounded opponent as a fierce wild boar. Even though or because he is wounded, his fiercest attack may be about to come.

You can be sure that your opponent, once wounded, will be more on key than before. Don't make the mistake of trying the same attack a second time. He will be ready for it and will take the opportunity to draw you in and cut you down.

Reclaiming the mind means keeping your mind and body working in unison, seamlessly, with neither getting ahead or out of time with the other. Stay ready and always be aware of the opponent's condition. Once he is wounded, keep your mind and sword flowing freely. Strike him again and again from all directions so that he cannot so much as lift his head; this is the highest level of a free-flowing mind. This is what is meant by striking at a hairsbreadth. Do not allow the opponent the time to move even a hairsbreadth between your first, second, and third cuts.

In the Zen philosophy of the battlefield of the mind the master strives to answer a question before a hairsbreadth of time has passed. In martial arts this is true also. If you hesitate you will die; there is no doubt about this outcome. Your weapon and your mind are one; allow no gap between action and reaction.

Purge the Mind, Sense the Void, and Center the Psyche

To purge the mind is to do away with all sickness in one instant. By sickness here I mean sickness of the mind. I described the various sicknesses of the mind earlier in the book. Remember, a sickness is anything that causes the mind to stop on any one point. For a Buddhist, this is known as seizing the mind, and it is avoided at all cost, because if the mind is seized by a thought it will not be free to absorb and respond to what is happening in the instant, and that will get you killed. The idea of purging is to cleanse the mind of all sickness at one time rather than searching for each individual sickness and risk overlooking the only one.

The meaning of "the only one" is a secret which must be taught in person. It is a reference to the mind of an opponent which has neither shape, color, nor size and is therefore a void. Knowing the void, or the only one, is knowing the mind of the opponent.

The entire point of Buddhism is to come to the understanding that the mind is void, but even among those who strictly adhere to the principles of Buddhism there are not many enlightened.

To center the psyche is to concentrate on the subtle signals that reveal the opponent's mind, chiefly his grip on the sword. Watch his grip, anticipate his move and beat him to the strike. A centered psyche can read an opponent's intention before he even knows what he is about to do. Purge the mind and center the psyche, read the opponent's mind correctly, interpreting his subtle movements, mainly his hands. To read his intentions as the thought is forming in his mind and strike before he can execute the move is known as striking the mind. The mind cannot move because it has no form or shape. Striking the opponent as the thought is formed but before the body can respond is in essence striking the mind.

This is a central point in the philosophy of Buddhism. There are two kinds of void, true and false. A false void is only nothingness. A true void is an unobstructed mind. Even though the mind is void of form and movement it is nevertheless the master of the entire body. Every little movement the body makes originates in the mind. Therefore, every action the opponent takes must start with his mind.

Now, a mind that is seized is void, but a void that is free flowing is a mind. The void moves freely, turns into a mind and controls the movements of the body. Since you should strike between thought and action, before the hands flinch, the technique is known as striking the mind.

We talk of reading the mind, but the mind is invisible. It is called void precisely because it has no shape or movement. But the mind is read through the movements of the hands that grip the blade, even though the mind itself is not seen. Strike after the command to move leaves the mind but before the body can execute it. The mind presents its intentions in many different ways, such as subtle hand movements, the positioning of the feet, shifts in weight, and countless other things.

It is impossible to learn this by reading a book, and listening to teachers will only get you so far. Too many teachers only repeat what they have been taught and are not enlightened at all.

True Enlightenment is a Rare Thing

Given that all human actions and deeds, even the most spectacular, are regulated by the dictates of the mind, it follows that the entire universe is also controlled by the mind of Heaven. At the bidding of the mind of Heaven there is thunder and lightning, blowing wind and rain, cloud formations, and ice, all in season and out of season, that perplex humanity.

The controlling mind of Heaven is a void, just as the human mind is a void. One is the Master of the universe and the other the master of each individual human being. Whether the human is a professional dancer, actor, warrior, marksman, or in any other profession that requires mastery, it is the mind of the individual that is the true master. If the mind is twisted then the body cannot hit the mark or achieve excellence.

When one has achieved a free-flowing mind, his body is centered and works as one with the dictates of his mind. Then he is free to excel in any area he chooses. It is the highest achievement to attain this kind of mind. Many people think they have come to enlightenment and use their minds to its fullest ability, but in truth there are very few who do. It is easy for an enlightened mind to see those who are not enlightened.

An enlightened mind cuts through the barriers and goes directly to the root of a problem. Those who beat around the bush and second guess themselves can hardly be considered enlightened. A direct, free-flowing, centered mind is known as a true mind or a natural mind. A twisted, diseased, and second-guessing mind is known as a false mind or a normal human mind. A person who has achieved a free-flowing mind and is one in his thoughts and actions is truly amazing.

I do not speak as one who has achieved this state. I find it hard to act in the consistent manner of a direct free-flowing mind, but I understand the way and I write according to that knowledge. That said, in the martial arts it is impossible for your fighting techniques to react according to the situation so long as your mind is not free and your body is not working instantly in accord with the dictates of the mind. You may do well in everyday life without the attainment of this enlightenment, but in combat, or the way of the warrior, it is crucial.

Even if you have attained a free mind in the martial arts and your mind and body work as one, it will still require a lot of hard work to apply that knowledge to everything. One who can do this is known as gifted. A master may have accomplished complete unity with his art, but that does not necessarily mean he is gifted.

The True Mind and the False Mind

A poem goes:

> It is your mind that confounds your mind
> Mind, do not yield to the mind

These lines speak of the conflict between the true mind and the false mind. Once one has attained their true, or free, mind and acts in accord with its dictates, everything that he does will be direct and to the heart of the situation. But if one begins to second guess himself and allows the false mind to distort the true mind, then everything he does will be distorted and false.

When we speak of the true and false mind we are not talking about two different minds—they are one and the same. The true mind is that part of you that exists in eternity, aware and functional before the birth of even your parents. The false mind is that part of the nature which is corrupted by birth and the introduction of the flesh. Your flesh was formed by the union of your parents, but it is obvious that the mind has no shape and was not created by human beings. The mind inhabits the body at birth and connects the natural with the supernatural.

The study of Zen is an effort to connect with the original mind. But many supposed Zen masters do nothing more than repeat things that they have heard and create a false sense of enlightenment even though they themselves are not enlightened.

When we speak of the false mind we are talking about that part of the flesh which causes the emotions to overwhelm reason. The flowing of the blood is different for each person and is therefore particular. When you are angry, the blood rushes to your face and turns it red as the emotion shows through. If someone despises what you love, you become angry and resent that person; but on the other hand, if someone values the same things you will feel a kinship and this may lead to a distortion of truth based only on agreement with a like mind. If someone is given a valuable gift it will cause him to feel gratitude and his blood will flow with emotion, and this feeling of gratitude may cause him to question what he believes is true. These are examples of how each individual's flesh is enticed in different ways, according to what they value, and reactions based on these differences are known as the consequences of the false mind.

When a person is led by his emotions, the false mind battles with the true mind to influence his actions. This always leads to bad outcomes. An enlightened person has learned to override his emotions with his true mind and therefore he deserves much deference. The unenlightened are not so, because they have clouded the judgment of the true mind and cause many blunders by following the false mind. These gain a reputation as shifty people.

The poem above is not holy writ, but it does distinguish good from evil. Everything the false mind does is evil by nature. If the false mind influences your actions, your martial prowess will fail, your aim will be false, and you will not be able to freely ride a horse, dance, or sing. Your words will be colored with emotion and false statements will proceed. Everything will be false because all your words and actions are based in a false mind. The true mind, on the other hand, will give forth true statements and everything will be true because it is based in the true mind.

Certain individuals will make false claims and argue against truth because their own emotions and desires shade their minds; their intentions can be readily seen. The truth is easily heard also. When the true mind speaks it is clear even without explanation or debate. A false mind is diseased. If you are to be successful in the martial arts you must purge your mind of the influence of the flesh, and then you will have a free-flowing mind.

This is true of all paths.

No Sword

The concept of No Sword is more centered on surviving a fight even though you have no sword than it is taking the sword from an opponent. This art is not meant to build up your reputation by making a show of how easily you can take a sword from your opponent. The focus should be on winning, not on taking the sword.

The art itself is not about grappling over what the opponent is intent on keeping; in fact, the art is equally centered on not trying to take a sword away from someone who is desperate to keep it. Remember, if you keep the opponent focused on trying to maintain a hold on his sword, he will not be focused on trying to cut you down. This is the essence of the art. If you keep his focus on this and avoid being cut down, then you win.

The art of fighting without a sword is not a simple compiling of techniques designed to wrist a sword away, but it is the art of using whatever means necessary to prevail in such a fight. If you can engage an armed opponent and take his weapon from him to use as your own, then you should be able to use anything at hand as a weapon also. Even a simple fan can be a deadly weapon against a sword in the hands of one so skilled. This is the real essence of the art. One proficient in this art should be able to win against an opponent armed with a long sword even if he is caught by surprise while taking a walk with only a bamboo stick. You should approach this art with this aim in mind.

The art of No Sword is not necessarily an art of killing. It is used when an opponent is determined to cut you down and will not be dissuaded. At that point, you may take his sword, but even though you disarm him this should be what your mind is focused on. The key to the art is the understanding of distancing. If you control the distance then there is no need to fear a sword, no matter how determined the opponent is to cut you down. Now, there is safety in staying far enough away that the opponent cannot strike you, but you can never take a sword away unless you close the distance, invade his space of safety, and lay hold on it. You must open yourself to danger in order to disarm the opponent.

The art of No Sword is in essence engaging an armed opponent with nothing but your empty hands as weapons. Since the opponent has the reach advantage with a long weapon you must be willing to fight him in close quarters. Practice the various ways your hands can be an advantage. Use evasion techniques and close the distance to lay hold on his sword handle. Move swiftly, grab surely. Do not fight for control of the blade; move to his side and take it away. Unless you are very close to him you will fail to take control.

The art of No Sword is a closely-guarded secret of this school. Postures, guards, distancing, movement, and strategy are all central to the art of No Sword.

Form and Function

For everything that has form there is a function, and nothing that has form is without purpose. Take the bow. It has a form, yet its function is in the drawing, aiming, and shooting of the arrow. A lamp has form, yet its purpose is the light it gives off. Water has a form, but hydration is its function. A plum tree has form, but bright color and sweet fragrance are its function. The sword has a form, but cutting, slashing, and the taking of life are its function.

The human body has a form and its function is the capacity for unlimited energy. Its purpose is whatever the mind chooses from an endless number of choices. In the same way that a plum tree has a form and gives off colorful flowers and sweet fragrance as a function of what is already contained within the form, the human uses the energy of the mind to accomplish whatever he chooses. For the warrior, this includes all manner of deception in combat: feigning, cutting, distancing, offense, and defense are all manifest externally in the movements of the body. The energy is within. The manifestation in physical form is the function.

It is possible for a human being to reach spiritual unity and achieve Heavenly results. When a monk reaches a level of complete reaction, in harmony with all his surroundings, is at one with any situation, and speaks from the depths of truth even in his off-handed comments, it is said that he has attained Heavenly aptitude and is at one with the will of Heaven. Being at one with the will of Heaven is not to say being controlled by a powerful spirit; rather, it refers to the state when one is free to react instantly and correctly to any given situation.

A Master is a person who has completed the circle of training and is no longer bound by the countless techniques, strategies, weapons, and hand strikes, but is free from the training so that he can react and interact effectively with any technique he has ever seen without the slightest thought to what he is doing. Unless you find the energy within, this level of excellence will not reveal itself.

Even while you are resting indoors, look up, left, and right, and stay alert of all around you in case something falls on you unexpectedly from above. If you are resting next to a door, make sure it is stable and will not fall over on you. If you are attending a high-ranking noble, you should remain prepared for any unexpected occurrence. Remain highly aware of your surroundings even when you are walking in and out of a doorway.

There are many examples of extraordinary energy fulfilled. An enlightened warrior living with a free mind will accomplish amazing acts instantly and appropriately to any situation. This is a high achievement. But before the energy matures, even though it is there, it is useless. In any path one embarks upon with great energy he must continually practice and train in order for his energy to become reality. If you rely on your energy alone, or become sidetracked, what was a great energy becomes a great obstacle, and all further progress will halt. But if you remain flexible and diligent, your energy will grow through out your mind and body until you are one with your path, and every part of your being will work in perfect unity.

If you cross paths with a warrior who is one with his art, regardless of the countless techniques you have memorized, you will not be able to so much as lift a finger against him. Such a one can freeze opponents in place with the power of his stare and cause the opponent to forget even to draw his sword. Like a cat fixing his gaze on a mouse, where the mouse is stricken to the point it forgets to run, so is the average warrior against one unified with his art. A man such as this is beyond the mental limits or possibilities of others. In every path there is learning and convention, but the master rises above learning and reshapes conventional thought. He is free from all limitation and acts in accord with a way that is beyond the understanding of others.

The energy strives to remain watchful of all things at all times, and if you are not careful it will consume you and trap you in a state of watchfulness rather than reaction. Because the energy is not harnessed and flowing throughout your entire body, the body will not respond properly even though the energy is alert. You must continuously perform exercises until every part of your being is at one with the energy. Then you will be in perfect unity with your path.

The energy is the doorway to the power of the mind. Energy is readily available in any situation, but it is always the servant of the mind, which is indeed the master of the entire body, even though it resides deep within. Energy unites the mind and body to accomplish any bidding of the mind—evil from an evil mind, and good from a good mind. The energy itself is neutral and can accomplish marvelous deeds or petty actions. It all depends on what is locked away in the mind.

There is one energy, whether we call it mental energy or physical energy, and it serves to unify our mind and actions. Even though we speak of the door to the mind, there is no physical place in the body where it is located. Think of it like a speech given by a master. The speech has a beginning and an end but the words themselves have no physical location.

The Fluid Mind

The great Master Manura said, "The mind changes countless times in every situation, yet every turning point is hardly visible to us."

This cryptic Zen saying is very difficult to grasp for a non-Zen student, but I repeat it here because of its extreme importance to the art of the sword. In the martial arts, the mind must change countless times to adapt to whatever the opponent is doing in the instance. If the opponent lifts his sword your mind must make adjustments accordingly; if he moves it to the left or right, appropriate adjustments must be made for that also. So we see the application of the first line of the poem. But the heart and soul of the martial arts is found in the second line, "Every turning point is hardly visible." The traces of where the mind has been fades out like the ripples in the water behind a boat. The boat continues to move forward without giving any attention to the ripples. So the mind of the warrior must continually adapt to what is ahead, without lingering on the ripples of the past, if he is to survive.

If your mind stops at any given point in the fluidity that is combat, you will die on the spot.

The mind has no form, shape, or color and is therefore invisible to the eye, but the actions caused in the body by the mind are visible to all. It is like cloth died red—it appears red. Likewise, if your mind is attracted to promiscuity, people will see it. Whatever the mind harbors, the actions of the body tell. If your mind stops in combat, the opponent will see it and kill you.

Although there is more to the poem above, I chose to quote only the first two lines, as I think they are most appropriate to the martial arts. If you are interested in learning more of it you should follow up in your study of Zen.

The Sword and Religious Philosophy

There are many principles of the sword that are also found in Buddhist and Zen teachings. Chiefly, there is the avoidance of attaching the mind to any one specific thing. This is a central concept and vitally important.

A woman wrote the following poem to Saigyo the priest;

> Once you have left home
> Your mind should not linger
> On the home you left

As a warrior, you should meditate on the last part of this poem. No matter how many secret techniques you have learned, if your mind lingers on a single one in battle you will die. Never allow your mind to dwell on any one thing—not the opponent, yourself, or your sword.

Between Things That Are and Things That Are Not

A Zen master said, "Do not see things in things that are, and do not see things in things that are not. Move beyond these things and see the truth behind."

This saying is germane for every path we walk, especially the path of the warrior. The things that are and the things that are not are the same as personal convictions of right and wrong, good and evil, which stand as pillars. To focus your mind on good is bad enough but to focus on evil is worse. The warrior should not focus on either because they can both cause the mind to fixate. It is vital for the warrior to have a mind free of preoccupation so that it is ever ready to react. Stand between the things that are and the things that are not and you will rise to the highest point between the two. Once you are a master you understand the power of seeing between the things that are and the things that are not.

Between Truth and Untruth

Focus not on truth or untruth. Once you have come to a truth do not let it bind you. Once you have truly learned a thing you should forget what you have learned and absorb the truth as part of you, not keep it as an object lesson in the mind. Once you have come full circle on a path, if you linger on the learning you will be bound by the truth that was meant to set you free, to say nothing of dwelling on untruth. If even truth should be removed from your active mind, how much more should untruth.

The way of a master is to do all things without thought to anything. If you are dwelling on truth you will never be free to become one with truth. Free your mind and live in reaction from a neutral position. Until you can do this you are not one with your path.

We teach these lessons with the sword in mind, as that is our primary concern, but it applies to all paths equally. If you know your sword is in your hand when you draw it, then your mind is not free from thought. If you see the arrow, then your mind is not free to hit the target. If your mind is free of knowledge of the sword or arrow then you are free to let excellence happen. The natural state of the mind is capable of accomplishing anything, but if your mind is diseased you will not be confident in speech or action.

The natural mind is one that has absorbed all learning and is free from any thought of all that it has learned.

From the Author

And so we conclude *The Warrior Series*, at least for now. I am anxious to finish several novels that I have been working on for several years. I suppose my writing style is a little unusual in that I write what I feel at the moment rather than laboring through one book at a time. That is why I have so many partially-finished works in progress. I suppose I enjoy it that way.

I am not sure if I am going to add any more volumes to this series, but I will certainly write more on the subject. I will write *The Warrior Manifesto* next. This will be an original work and it will be good to get back to my own voice. As any good warrior, I have a duty to my Lord, and I will try to fulfill that in several other books that I have planned.

It has been a real pleasure spending this time with you, and I hope the things I have recorded here are of some value to you. As I have said before, it is for each of us to choose our own path. Choose wisely. Follow the dictates of your own soul regardless of what others may say. If history has taught us anything, it's that the truly great have a mind of their own.

Be Great!!!

D. E. Tarver

0-595-27998-8

51258857R00040

Made in the USA
Lexington, KY
18 April 2016